Roanoa

Trinety harbor

Hatorasck

PRIMARY SOURCES OF THE THIRTEEN COLONIES AND THE LOST COLONY™

A Primary Source History of the Colony of
NORTH CAROLINA

PHILLIP MARGULIES

rosen central
Primary Source™

The Rosen Publishing Group, Inc., New York

Published in 2006 by The Rosen Publishing Group, Inc.
29 East 21st Street, New York, NY 10010

Library of Congress Cataloging-in-Publication Data

Margulies, Phillip, 1952–
A primary source history of the colony of North Carolina/by Phillip
Margulies.—1st ed.
    p. cm.—(Primary sources of the thirteen colonies and the lost colony)
Includes bibliographical references and index.
ISBN 1-4042-0432-6 (lib. binding)
ISBN 1-4042-0666-3 (pbk binding)
1. North Carolina—History—Colonial period, ca. 1600–1775—Juvenile literature.
2. North Carolina—History—1775–1865—Juvenile literature.
I. Title. II. Primary sources in American history (New York, N.Y.)
F254.3M35 2006
975.6—dc22

                                                                        2004022723

Manufactured in the United States of America

On the cover: This sixteenth-century drawing by Theodore de Bry depicts the walls of a fortress in Carolina.

CONTENTS

INTRODUCTION

Into the Unknown

Early in the sixteenth century, the people of Europe realized that explorer Christopher Columbus had not found a route to the fabled Spice Islands of Asia during his voyages across the Atlantic Ocean beginning in 1492. Instead, he had found something more interesting and potentially even more lucrative—two giant landmasses that were not recorded on any map. After a while, Europeans started referring to the continents of North and South America as the New World. It is difficult today to comprehend how appropriate that expression was, how strange and vast the sparsely populated lands must have seemed to the first Europeans who tried to settle there. In twenty-first century terms, it would be like discovering a nearby planet, rich in natural resources and able to sustain life, whose existence had previously escaped the notice of astronomers.

Within 100 years of Columbus's first voyage across the Atlantic Ocean, the first colonists came to North Carolina. They sailed on ships that were prey to storms that could wreck them or blow them hundreds of miles off course. It was a breathtaking leap into the unknown. In those days, when people crossed the Atlantic to America, they left everything they had ever known—home, family, friends, security. In all probability, they would never again see the loved ones they had left behind. That was the only near-certainty in a risky adventure that was full of unknowns.

The story of North Carolina is a tale of great ocean-crossing migrations. Yet it is also the saga of overland migrations undertaken

Christopher Columbus is depicted in this 1594 color engraving by Theodor de Bry, an engraver and publisher from the Netherlands who worked in Frankfurt, Germany. De Bry published and provided art for a large multi-volume history of voyages to the New World. This engraving is thought to be based on an original portrait of Columbus painted before the explorer's first voyage to the Americas and commissioned by the king and queen of Spain. They wanted something to remember Columbus by should he not return alive. The original portrait that this engraving is based on is thought to be one of the few of Columbus actually painted during his lifetime.

by hardy pioneers from other American colonies who pushed their way south into the backcountry of North Carolina to find better territory to settle. People of many different classes and backgrounds—from slave to aristocrat—made these perilous journeys. They changed the country they came to, and in turn, they were changed by it. From out of a diverse group of adventurers and pioneers, there eventually emerged a unified citizenry—the people of the proud state of North Carolina.

CHAPTER 1

Explorers and Colonists

In 1524, King Francis I of France looked enviously at the Spanish conquests in America. Thirty-two years had passed since Christopher Columbus, looking for a direct sea route to Asia and its supposed wealth of gold, pearls, and spices, had discovered a New World unknown to the geographers of Europe. It was a world full of strange plants and animals, pyramid-building empires like those that had existed in ancient Egypt, and gold and silver mines. No one knew what else these vast new lands contained—maybe other empires to conquer or more gold to mine. Or maybe these lands really contained the direct sea route to the East that Columbus had sought. What Francis I did know was that Spain had claimed much of this territory with the help of its seafaring explorers.

French and Spanish Exploration of North Carolina

Whatever new discoveries were waiting to be made, Francis I wanted France to have a share in them. He hired a Florentine navigator named Giovanni da Verrazano to lead an expedition to the New World. Accompanied by his brother, Girolamo, who was a mapmaker, Verrazano led a crew of fifty men on his ship *La Dauphine* as they landed off what is now Cape Fear, North Carolina. Verrazano cautiously anchored at sea and went ashore by boat. There he met some native peoples, whom he later described as having reddish skin, similar to what was then considered a Middle Eastern complexion.

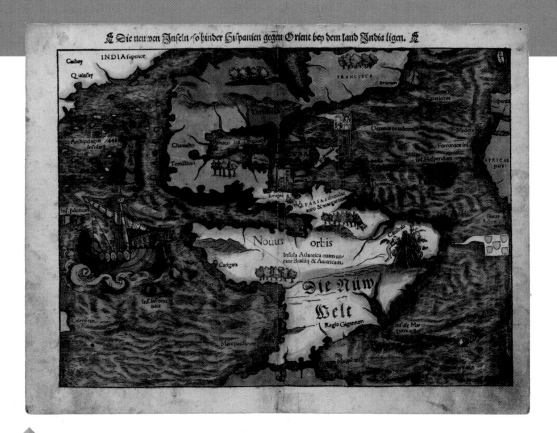

Sebastian Münster, an important sixteenth-century German cartographer, was the first mapmaker to publish separate maps of the world's continents, including this 1540 map of the American continent. Previously, maps of the Americas were included in large world maps. Labeled the "New World" in both Latin ("Novis orbis") and German ("die Nüw Welt"), the landmass also includes a reference to America, following the lead of another sixteenth century German cartographer, Martin Waldseemüller, who was the first to use the term on a map in 1507. This map repeats Verrazano's error in confusing North Carolina's Pamlico Sound with the Pacific Ocean in its depiction of the Outer Banks.

Continuing his voyage, Verrazano sailed north and reached the Outer Banks—the long, narrow barrier islands that stand between the Atlantic Ocean and almost the entire Carolina coast. Here, he and his mapmaker brother made a serious geographical error. They thought Pamlico Sound, the waterway between the Outer Banks and mainland North America, was the Pacific Ocean. As a result, for nearly a century afterward, maps of North America showed the continent divided in two—a pair of giant landmasses connected on the East Coast by a tiny strip of land we now know as the Outer Banks.

Sailing north again, Verrazano came to a place so lovely he called it Arcadia, named after a pastoral region in ancient Greece. It it now believed to be present-day Kitty Hawk, North Carolina. At this spot, Verrazano abducted a young Native American child and tried to kidnap a young Native American woman as well (perhaps intending to take them back to Europe with him). Afterward, he went on to explore New York Harbor and the coast of Maine. He made two more voyages to America and died in 1528 at the hands of a tribe of Caribs on an island southeast of Puerto Rico named Guadalupe.

The next Europeans to find their way to North Carolina were Spaniards marching north from Florida during Hernando de Soto's expedition in search of gold. Led by Native American guides, de Soto entered southwestern North Carolina in 1540. He and his men stayed for about a month. They did not find any gold, so they moved south toward present-day Alabama, Mississippi, and Arkansas.

From 1566 to 1567, Juan Pardo, another Spanish explorer, was also looking for gold and led an expedition to North Carolina. Like those before him, Pardo left no permanent settlement. After a while the Spanish determined that there was not much of value in the region and decided to stop sending explorers to the area. This opened the door to British colonization of much of the eastern coast of the present-day United States.

Sir Walter Raleigh and the First English Colonies

In 1578, Britain began to plant colonies in North America. That year, Queen Elizabeth I granted a charter to Sir Humphrey Gilbert to settle any lands in America that were not already claimed by any other "Christian prince or people," namely Spain. When Gilbert died in a storm in 1583, Elizabeth transferred the charter to his half brother, Walter Raleigh.

The first North American expedition sent by Raleigh, which was exploratory in nature, reached the North Carolina coast near present-day Hatteras in 1584. It then moved north, probably to Roanoke Island. Commanded by Sir Richard Grenville and led by Philip Amadas and Arthur Barlowe, the expedition approached the exploration more scientifically and methodically than earlier explorers. Raleigh's men collected plants, rocks, and soil samples to send back to England. They also took back two Native American men, Manteo and Wanchese, who willingly accompanied the ship as it returned to England. Raleigh wanted to show Elizabeth and her subjects these men as examples of the nearly thirty Native American groups that lived on the land that would become North Carolina.

The interest that these friendly Native Americans attracted, together with enthusiastic reports of the new land and its abundant resources, helped Raleigh raise money for a second expedition in 1585. This time the expedition was designed to establish a permanent colony in present-day North Carolina. Raleigh sent 600 colonists under the leadership of Sir Richard Grenville. When the colonists reached Roanoke Island in April 1585, they started Britain's first American colony by building a settlement named Fort Raleigh.

In late August, Grenville returned to England, leaving more than 100 men behind under the leadership of a captain named Ralph Lane. After angering the neighboring Roanoke Indians by raiding their main village, stealing their supplies, and murdering their chief, Lane and the other colonists abandoned the settlement and returned to England. They set sail with Sir Francis Drake, who was on his way back to England after attacking Spanish strongholds in Florida and the Spanish West Indies. Meanwhile, Grenville returned

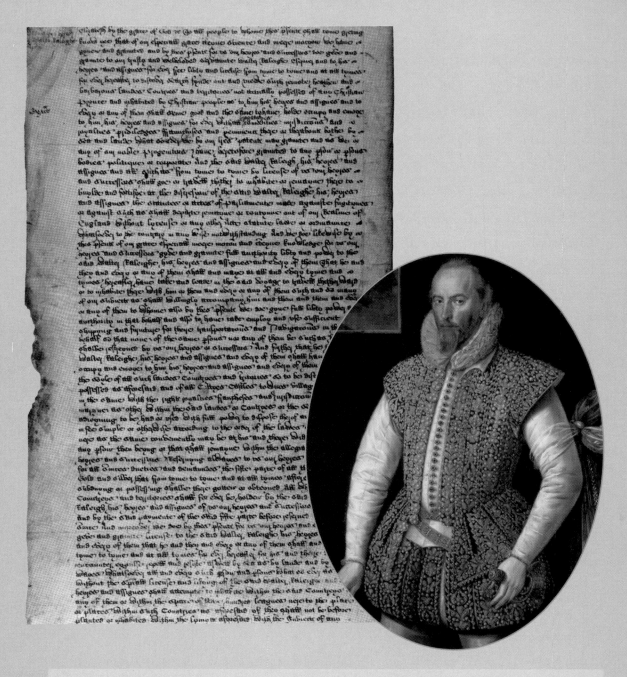

On March 25, 1584, Queen Elizabeth I granted poet and explorer Sir Walter Raleigh a charter *(left)* to explore and settle land in the New World on behalf of England. Raleigh prepared an expedition, led by Philip Amadas and Arthur Barlowe. These men arrived in Pamlico Sound in present-day North Carolina and landed on Roanoke Island. Their enthusiastic description of the land's bounty led to the establishment of a colony on Roanoke the next year. Raleigh appears above right in an anonymous sixteenth-century portrait. See the charter's transcription on page 53.

to the colony with three supply ships in the summer of 1586 and found that all of the colonists had disappeared. Returning to England once again, he left behind fifteen men to guard Fort Raleigh from further mishap.

Undaunted by this failure, Raleigh proceeded to plan a second colonizing expedition to North Carolina in 1587. Led by the planned colony's appointed governor, artist John White, 150 settlers, including 17 women and 9 children, arrived near Hatteras in June 1587. Soon they traveled on to Roanoke Island, where they established what became known as the White Colony. On Roanoke, they found some of the houses built by Ralph Lane's party still standing. On August 18, 1587, White's daughter, Eleanor Dare, gave birth to Virginia Dare, the first British child born in America.

The White Colony was both a tragic failure and a mystery. The colonists arrived too late in the growing season to plant crops, so provisions for the first winter in the New World were scanty. A looming naval war between Britain and Spain blocked shipping lanes and prevented the colony from being resupplied until 1590. When White—who had gone back to England to get supplies—was finally able to return, the colonists were gone. Since their bodies were never found, no one knows for certain what happened to the settlers of the lost colony. One of the few clues left behind was the word "CROATOAN" carved on a tree. The Croatoans were one of the almost thirty Native American tribes living in the area. There was also Croatoan Island 50 miles (80 km) from Roanoke. Later, Chief Powhatan of the Algonquins (and the father of Pocahontas, who became famous for saving the life of John Smith of the later Jamestown Colony in Virginia) told the Jamestown colonists that the White Colony settlers had

Native Americans dance in a circle in this sixteenth-century lithograph based on a drawing by John White, the leader of the so-called White Colony, the second attempted colonization of Roanoke Island by the English. Originally, White and his colonists were supposed to settle along Chesapeake Bay, but, after crossing the Atlantic, the pilot of their ship refused to take them any farther than Roanoke Island. Following an emergency voyage to England to obtain desperately needed supplies, White returned to Roanoke to find that his colony had vanished. After an unsuccessful search for survivors, White began heading back to England and Ireland and may have died at sea in 1606.

been caught in the middle of a war between two rival bands of Native Americans.

The Lords Proprietors of North Carolina

In 1663, King Charles II of Great Britain and Ireland wanted to reward eight men who had helped him gain the throne following

North Carolina came very close to being the site of England's first permanent settlement in America, but in the end it was not. The Barrier Islands near the coast of North Carolina made it hard to establish good harbors where ships could safely come and go. In fact, the treacherous Carolina coast wrecked so many ships, it became known as the "graveyard of the Atlantic." Since the first colonists had to arrive and be resupplied by sea, the absence of good harbors was a serious disadvantage. The Virginia coastline, by contrast, has harbors perfect for disembarking people safely on land and shipping goods in and out.

As a result of these geographical considerations, Britain's first successful colonies were planned in Virginia. North Carolina was gradually settled not so much by people sailing from Britain as from those wandering south from other British colonies in North America. Starting in the 1650s, colonists who were already accustomed to the hard frontier life migrated south to North Carolina in search of more and better land. By the early 1700s, many of them were coming from Pennsylvania and Virginia. Since the exact date of the first permanent settlement is unknown, North Carolina is sometimes called "the state without a birthday."

the English civil wars. His father, King Charles I, was executed after the conflict and the forces of the antimonarchists created a military dictatorship to rule Britain. Having gained the throne, Charles II named his eight friends as the lords proprietors of an enormous tract of land that stretched southward from the present-day Virginia-Carolina state line down to Florida (including land claimed by the Spanish) and westward to the "south seas." This vast territory was named Carolina in honor of his father, Charles I. "Carolus" is the Latin form of "Charles."

The lords proprietors of Carolina were given power to create and fill offices, establish courts of justice, collect taxes, confer titles of nobility, raise an army, and wage war. In theory, at least, they had a lot of power. Enforcing their rule on widely scattered, fiercely independent colonists spread throughout a vast land was another matter. The previously established and self-governing colonists saw the lords proprietors as outsiders and did not like what they had in mind for the colony.

According to their charter from the king, the lords proprietors were entitled to rule their domains like feudal lords. They hoped to duplicate in America the way of life that had held sway in Britain for centuries. There would be noblemen with titles; "freeman" could buy and sell property and leave the land if and when they wished. Other colonists would be like medieval serfs, bound to the land and in servitude to its owner or landlord. At the bottom of this colonial society would be slaves who could be bought, sold, and forced to work without payment or freedom of any kind.

However, the lords proprietors of Carolina arrived on the scene too late to impose this social order on the settlement. Colonial North Carolina could not be called a bastion of freedom—there were slaves, as well as indentured servants who worked for a master for a specific period of time before earning their freedom. But for white settlers, at least, it was a far more democratic place than Britain. The restrictive laws the proprietors tried to impose were resisted or ignored. As the years passed and their feudal dreams remained unfulfilled, the proprietors and their successors began to rule as absentee landlords and appointed a series of corrupt, incompetent governors to oversee the colony.

During this time, another part of Carolina began to be developed south of the Albemarle region that was the earliest site of

The Charter of 1663, pictured here, was granted to the eight lords proprietors of Carolina by English king Charles II as a reward for supporting him during his successful attempt to gain the throne. The charter represents the first attempt at an organized representative government in colonial Carolina. It allowed for the creation of an assembly composed of representatives of the colony's freemen; it guaranteed the colonists the full rights of English citizens, including property ownership; and it established a court system. Religious tolerance was also called for in the charter. A small ink sketch of Charles II appears in the document's top left corner. See the transcription on page 53.

colonial settlement. In 1657, Nathaniel Batts built a house at the western end of Albemarle Sound, making him the first-known European to permanently settle in North Carolina. Its development soon eclipsed that of the northern areas of the Carolina colony because it had a natural harbor and offered easier access to trade with the West Indies. From 1692 to 1712, North and South Carolina shared a single government. The colonial assembly and council were in North Carolina, while the governor lived in Charleston, South Carolina. A deputy governor was appointed to oversee affairs in North Carolina.

In 1729, seven of the eight lords proprietors sold their shares of North Carolina to King George II of England. The Crown began to rule North Carolina directly as a royal colony, and it remained that way until the American Revolution. The colony had a two-unit government composed of the governor and his council and a colonial assembly of representatives elected by the colony's voters. All colonial officials who were once appointed by the lords proprietors—including the governor and his council—were now appointed by the Crown.

CHAPTER 2

The People of Colonial North Carolina

Historians and anthropologists estimate that around 30,000 Native Americans were living in North Carolina when the first English explorers and colonists began to arrive. Their population may have been several times greater a few generations earlier, when the Spanish explorer Hernando de Soto first encountered them.

One important source of information about the customs of North Carolina's original inhabitants are the drawings and observations made by artist and Roanoke governor John White. Native Americans were organized into tribes, each with its own chief and own language. Some thirty tribes resided in North Carolina. The most important were the Hatteras, the Chowanocs, the Tuscaroras, the Catawbas, and the Cherokees. They were skillful farmers, growing corn, potatoes, tobacco, beans, peas, and many other vegetables. Domesticated animals were scarce in America before the arrival of Europeans and their horses, hogs, and cattle, but wild game was plentiful. North Carolina's Native Americans got their meat from hunting wild deer, bear, rabbits, birds, and fish. In most tribes, women did the planting and cooking. They made clothes and cared for the children. Women also made mats and baskets from grass reeds and rushes. Men hunted and fought when war broke out between tribes. Native Americans lived near their crops in small

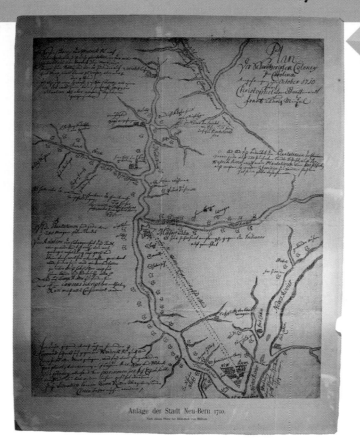

Anlage der Stadt Neu-Bern 1710.

The Carolina town of New Bern was settled by Swiss and German adventurers led by Baron Christopher von Graffenried from Bern, Switzerland. Von Graffenried drew this map of the settlement at New Bern, in present-day North Carolina, in October 1710. The Neuse and Trent rivers are pictured, as well as the houses that had been built along their banks, some of which are specifically identified. New Bern, situated where the two rivers meet, is the second-oldest town in North Carolina.

villages and towns. Some of their houses were round tents, while others were more solid, permanent structures covered with cypress or pine bark.

Early European Settlers

In the late 1600s and early 1700s, most of the settlers in North Carolina were of English descent. Most had reached North Carolina by way of Virginia. Many of these former Virginians were former indentured servants or the children of indentured servants—people who had agreed to work for a period of time to pay for their passage to the New World. By moving to North Carolina, they could start a new life in different surroundings, without anyone they had known before looking down on them for having once been servants.

Other European settlers came to North Carolina fleeing religious persecution. Among them were French Huguenots, disciples of Protestant leader John Calvin who had been driven out of France during the Wars of Religion. During that conflict, which occurred in the second half of the sixteenth century, thousands of French Protestants were murdered by royal soldiers, acting on behalf of France's Catholic Queen Mother, Catherine de Medici and her son, King Charles IX.

Other oppressed Protestant groups fled to the New World to escape religious persecution. In 1710, the town of New Bern, North Carolina, was founded by a colony of German Palatines. The Palatines were people of various Protestant denominations from the upper Rhine region of Germany. Also, members of the Quakers, another religious group that was discouraged in England, were among the early settlers in North Carolina. Most of the Quakers made their way to North Carolina from Pennsylvania.

The Highlanders

During the eighteenth century, the population of North Carolina expanded rapidly. In 1729, about 30,000 whites and fewer than 6,000 African slaves lived in the province. Less than fifty years later in 1775, the white population was estimated at 265,000 and the African population at 80,000. Most of the increase was due to immigration.

Many members of this new wave of immigrants came as a result of political and economic upheaval in Scotland. In 1707, the British parliament passed the Act of Union that would eventually make Scotland a part of Great Britain. Eventually the Scots took up arms to resist this alliance with Britain. In April 1746 at Culloden, the Scots were defeated. In the aftermath of the war, the Scottish clan system was broken up, Scottish estates were confiscated, and Scots were forbidden to bear arms and to wear the tartan (plaid) kilts that indicated their clan affiliation. British officers took over many Scottish estates, and by substituting sheep raising for farming, they put many Scots out of work.

The king offered to pardon all of the Scottish rebels who would take an oath of allegiance to the royal family and sail to America. Thousands of Scottish Highlanders—the rebellious and independent-minded clan members who lived in Scotland's mountainous areas—took advantage of this offer. As a result, a large wave of Scottish immigrants began entering North Carolina, a tide that continued right up until the American Revolution. Many Scots in North Carolina continued to speak Gaelic, their native language. In 1756, an observer reported that many of them knew almost no English. Most of the Highlander immigrants became farmers, though many became merchants.

The Scots

Another important immigrant group in colonial North Carolina was the so-called Scots (once referred to as the Scotch-Irish). The group was composed of descendants of Lowland Scots who had immigrated to Ulster, in what is now Northern Ireland, in the 1600s. They immigrated to Ireland with the encouragement of King James I of England, who installed them on land that had formerly belonged to Irish Catholic farmers. The Lowland Scots, like the English, were Protestants. King James hoped the Scots would give him greater control over the rebellious Catholic Irish, who resented Britain's attempts to rule their land and outlaw their religion. In Ireland, the transplanted Scots came to be referred to as Irish Protestants or Irish Presbyterians. When they later immigrated to the American colonies, they became known as the Scots.

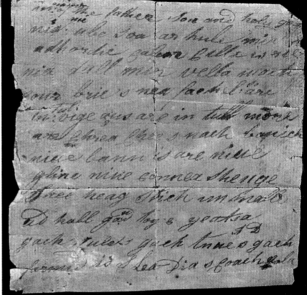

Many Scots immigrated to North Carolina following the battle of Culloden (1746). In this battle, Highlanders who supported the efforts of exiled Prince Charles Stewart to gain the English throne were defeated by English forces. In this eighteenth-century lithograph *(left)*, Gillies MacBean, a major in the Highland army, fights the better-armed and more numerous English. He would kill fourteen English soldiers before being killed himself. At right is a charm against evil written in Scots Gaelic and belonging to North Carolina settler Dougald McFarland. Even toward the end of the eighteenth century, Gaelic was still being spoken in Cumberland County and the upper Cape Fear Valley, where many of the Scots settled.

The Scots became prosperous in Ireland by developing sheep farms and woolen and linen manufacturing. They were so successful that English wool merchants objected to the competition they offered. To help the English merchants, Parliament passed the Woolen Act, which forbade the export of Irish wool and cloth to any places except England and Wales. This act was an economic blow to the Scots. Parliament also enacted other laws that discriminated against the Scots and other Protestants,

At left is a fraktur, an illustrated nineteenth-century family record written in German. It belonged to Philip Sell of North Carolina and documents the birth of his wife, Dorothea, on June 5, 1765, and her marriage to Philip in 1784. German-language frakturs were handwritten documents that recorded births and baptisms in the last half of the eighteenth century. "Fraktur" literally means "fractured writing." This refers to the ornate lettering style in which each letter remains separate from and unconnected to neighboring letters (unlike cursive lettering, for example). The text of frakturs was often surrounded and embellished by simple images of soldiers, angels, mermaids, birds, and animals.

including the Test Act, which excluded the Scots from holding civil and military offices and from practicing law in Great Britain and Ireland. More economic trouble occurred when a series of poor harvests led to famine in Ulster.

This combination of economic hard times and religious discrimination led to an exodus of Ulster Scots to America. Most Scots immigrants headed to Pennsylvania because of that colony's reputation for religious tolerance. As land in Pennsylvania became more expensive, however, these settlers moved south to North Carolina. Some Scots also moved to North Carolina directly from Scotland.

Germans and Czechs

In the early years of the eighteenth century, the region that is now Germany was part of a group of small kingdoms and principalities with different political organizations and religions. The Protestant Reformation—a religious reform movement that resulted in a sometimes violent break with Catholicism and the formation of various alternative Christian churches—had begun in this area in the sixteenth century, led by the former German Catholic monk Martin Luther. Germany had been the scene of the most bitter and violent fighting between Protestants and Roman Catholics.

Like the Scotch-Irish, Germans came to America seeking religious liberty, freedom from the Old World's religious wars, and economic opportunity. In addition, members of some German Protestant sects came to start self-contained religious communities and to perform missionary work among the Native Americans. Most of the German settlers in North Carolina belonged to the Lutheran, Reformed, or Moravian faiths. (The Moravians were followers of the Protestant martyr Jan Hus from Bohemia, which is now part of the present-day Czech Republic.) The Moravians often started experimental villages in North Carolina in which all property was held in common.

Africans

While many European colonists traveled to North Carolina in search of freedom, a large portion of the colony's population arrived in chains—the chains of slavery—beginning in the second half of the seventeenth century. Some Africans sailed directly to North Carolina aboard African slave ships. Others were born into slavery either in the North American colonies or in the Caribbean.

African slaves began appearing in North Carolina in the later 1600s. They mostly worked on small farms in the eastern part of the colony, planting and harvesting tobacco and corn crops and raising livestock. Because the terrain of much of North Carolina was either mountainous, swampy, or heavily forested, the land did not lend itself to the sprawling plantations established in the lower Southern colonies. Partly for this reason, slaveholding was less common in North Carolina than in the lower South. Roughly 28 percent of free households owned slaves (compared with 46 percent for South Carolina). This does not mean, however, that slaves in North Carolina were treated any better than elsewhere. The violence depicted in the nineteenth century woodcuts above would have been typical punishments administered to North Carolina slaves.

Most of the slaves in North Carolina lived and worked in the eastern part of the state on relatively small farms, growing tobacco, rice, and other crops.

The treatment of slaves was harsh to begin with and became even harsher as time went on. In the early days of the colony, some slaves were allowed to keep livestock and cultivate small plots of land for their own use. However, a law was passed in

1741 that forbade slaves to own livestock. Slaves were considered property, not people, and as such had no legal rights. They could not be tried in the same court as freemen and could not testify in court against white men. To prevent slaves from escaping, laws were passed that forbade slaves to travel without special passes. Slaves were not allowed to hunt or to possess firearms. They were forbidden to gather in groups for fear that they would plot rebellion or escape. For the same reason, they were not allowed to communicate with each other at night.

The punishments for breaking these rules were brutal. The law of 1741 that forbade slaves from owning livestock also said that slaves who were convicted of perjury (lying under oath) should have their ears cut off. The law stated that "It shall be lawful for any Person or Persons whatsoever to kill and destroy each Slave or Slave by such Ways and Means as he or she shall think fit, without Accusation or Impeachment of any Crime for the same," as quoted in Hugh Talmage Lefler's *North Carolina: The History of a Southern State*. It was not until 1774 that a law was passed making the "willful and malicious killing" of a slave by a white person a crime. The punishment that a white man received for killing a slave "maliciously" was only twelve months in prison.

Not all Africans in colonial North Carolina were slaves. As early as 1701 there was a small number of free blacks living in the colony. By 1790, the state of North Carolina had 5,000 free black citizens. Many free Africans were skilled artisans—carpenters, coopers, bricklayers, blacksmiths, spinners, weavers, and wheelwrights. Most were farmers, and a few acquired large properties.

CHAPTER 3

In the early part of the eighteenth century, North Carolina was still a raw frontier. The colony's first town, Bath, was not incorporated until 1706. North Carolina's interior was the scene of violent clashes between settlers and Native Americans. Its coastline was home to smugglers and pirates, including some whose names have passed into legend. These include the notorious Blackbeard and the "gentleman pirate," Stede Bonnet.

The Tuscarora War

The Native Americans of North Carolina recognized fairly early that the colonists were a threat to their interests, but they also realized that there was little they could do about it. John Lawson, an Englishman, wrote a book on his experiences in colonial North Carolina. Of the Native Americans, he observed: "They are really better to us than we have been to them." Settlers often bought land from the original inhabitants, but in many cases they did not pay what the Native Americans asked in compensation. Some whites made a practice of kidnapping Native Americans, particularly women and children, and selling them into slavery. Whites who traded with the Native Americans often cheated them.

European settlers had overwhelming advantages over the native peoples of North America. Many colonists had developed immunity to various epidemic diseases. Once introduced to the native population, however, these diseases killed many Native Americans. In addition, the settlers had better tools and weapons,

Untamed
North Carolina

Before the arrival of Europeans, Tuscarora Indians lived in the North Carolina Coastal Plain. Initially enjoying decent relations with the newly arriving settlers, the Tuscaroras eventually became angry over European trading practices. They were also upset over the capture and enslavement of tribe members and increasing encroachment upon their land. In early September 1711, some Tuscaroras captured New Bern founder Baron von Graffenried, John Lawson (North Carolina's surveyor general), and two African slaves. Eventually, Lawson was executed, but von Graffenried and the slaves were released unharmed. Von Graffenried made this sketch of the incident.

although native peoples purchased guns from traders as quickly as they could. The colonists could fight "hostile Indians" with the help of "friendly Indians" of other tribes. In this way, the settlers worsened the divisions between the tribes by playing them off one another and strengthening their own position in the process.

As a result of these advantages, in addition to ongoing immigration, European colonists soon came to outnumber the Native Americans. One of the last great stands made by eastern Native Americans against European colonists was that of the Tuscarora, one of the six groups in the large Iroquois tribe. The

The manner of their attire and painting them selves when they goe to their generall huntings or at theire Solemne feasts.

To the east of the Tuscarora lived the Algonquins of coastal North Carolina. The Algonquins had migrated south from the northeastern regions of the present-day United States and survived mainly through hunting, fishing, and gathering. The Carolina Algonquins included the Chowanoke, Weapemeoc, Poteskeet, Moratoc, Roanoke, Secotan, Pomeiooc, Neusiok, Croatoan, and Chesepiooc tribes. At left is a member of either the Secotan or Pomeiooc tribes, as painted by John White in the late sixteenth century. White was the leader of the doomed White Colony, the second attempted European colonization of Carolina.

Tuscaroras had probably planned their uprising for a long time. The tribe picked a moment when the whites were distracted by other problems, including a small-scale civil war. Called the Cary Rebellion, the civil war was fought over religion and waged between the supporters of a governor and former governor of the colony. The Tuscaroras knew about the disunity between the whites because both sides had been asking them for their support in the civil war. The colony had also been weakened by a series of bad harvests.

Early on the morning of September 22, 1711, numerous bands of Tuscaroras simultaneously attacked white settlements across a wide swath of the colony. Many of the victims were the families of traders known to the Tuscaroras. The initial attacks occurred within the space of a few hours, and, in this instance, the Tuscaroras were better armed than the settlers. Crops were burned and livestock slaughtered or carried away. Men, women, and children were killed and their bodies mutilated. Some women were laid on the floor of their homes with stakes driven through their hearts.

With much of the colony under attack, Edward Hyde, North Carolina's governor, applied for help from the Virginia colony to the north. Due to a border dispute between the two colonies, his request was denied. South Carolina, however, sent troops. The expedition against the Tuscaroras was led by Colonel John Barnwell, later known as Tuscarora Jack. Initially, the troops that marched against the Tuscaroras consisted of 30 whites from South Carolina, 250 North Carolina militia, and 500 "friendly Indians," mostly members of the Yemassees tribe who were not allied with the Tuscaroras. Armed with cannons, the colonists and their Native American allies laid siege to a Tuscarora fort where white women and children were being held captive. The Tuscaroras agreed to a truce. Under the terms of the truce, the Tuscaroras would release the captives and give up even more of their land.

North Carolina officials were not happy that Barnwell had made a truce with the Tuscaroras instead of destroying them. The North Carolina Assembly refused to give him a grant of land that he had requested as repayment for his services. Determined to profit from his efforts on behalf of North Carolina, Barnwell and his men kidnapped some Native Americans and took them as slaves to South Carolina. The Tuscaroras saw this as a violation of the truce and resumed their attacks. North Carolina was further weakened when a yellow fever epidemic struck, killing Governor Hyde among many others. Once again, South Carolina came to the assistance of its neighbor to the north.

In December 1712, South Carolina colonel James Moore marched into North Carolina with 33 colonists and about 1,000 allied Native Americans. Moore and acting North Carolina governor Thomas Pollock defeated the Tuscaroras at Fort Nohoroco on Contentea Creek on March 25, 1713. They inflicted the kind of punishment that the North Carolina Assembly had been hoping for earlier. Pollock reported the results: "Enemies Destroyed is as follows—Prissoners 392, Scolps 192, out of ye sd. fort-& att Least 200 Kill'd & Burnt In ye fort—I& 166 Kill'd & taken out of ye fort," as quoted by Lefler.

According to Governor Alexander Spotswood of Virginia, some of the Tuscarora captives were tortured to the point of death. Others were sold into slavery. The power of the Tuscaroras in North Carolina was broken. Most of the survivors moved out of the colony. Many of them moved to New York, homeland of the Iroquois.

Pirates of the Carolina Coast

Although people sometimes romanticize the heyday of pirates, the act of piracy was nothing more than the armed robbery of ships. The late 1600s and early 1700s were a golden age of piracy along the Carolina coast. Blackbeard and Stede Bonnet are two of the most famous pirates who operated in and around the Carolinas. At the time, piracy was so common in Carolina that it gave the colony and its government a bad reputation throughout the American colonies and in Europe. The British government accused Carolina's colonial government of sheltering pirates, encouraging their illegal activity, and sharing in their stolen booty.

In August 4, 1697, letter from the Lords Commissioners of the Council of Trade concerning piracy in the American colonies appears at right. In response to a complaint about the prevalence of piracy along the East Coast, a council official writes to request more information about the situation: "What are the names of the Pirates, and in what manner and by whom have they been entertained? About the Pirates that you say are gone from Boston, Rhode Island, New York, Pennsylvania, Carolina, and Barbados: Who are they who are concerned with them, and what are their designs?"

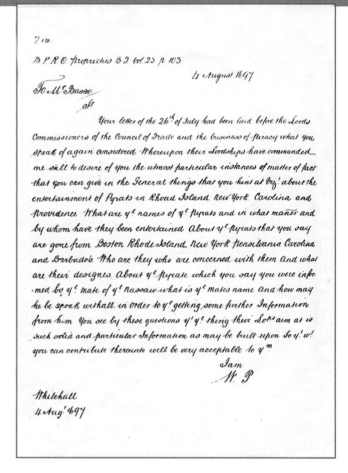

Piracy was common in North Carolina for several reasons. First, as the British rightly complained, piracy was tolerated by colonial officials. The notorious Blackbeard boasted that he could be invited into any home in North Carolina, and he was probably telling the truth. Many colonists viewed piracy as just the most extreme form of a kind of lawlessness that they did not consider unusual or even bad.

Piracy was linked to smuggling and privateering. Smuggling is the illegal trade of goods across borders. It is usually done in order to avoid government taxes on the legitimate buying and selling of those goods or to import or export goods considered illegal by the government. In colonial times, the British government put taxes on goods sold in the colonies in order to increase the colonies' profitability to the mother country. Britain also tried to prevent the colonists from selling certain goods to its enemies and competitors—such as France, Spain, and Holland—and discouraged the colonists from buying many goods from countries other than Britain, even if the colonists could get them cheaper elsewhere. After all, Britain had founded the colonies, funded them, and sent soldiers to defend them in time of war. The British reasoned that in return they should reap the benefits of trade with the colonies.

The trouble was that during hard economic times, obeying Britain's trade regulations would have ruined the colonists. To avoid poverty, colonists regularly disobeyed the rules. Many colonists recognized that smuggling was illegal, but they justified it as an issue of economic survival. This kind of thinking led to toleration of other forms of lawlessness, including piracy.

The boundary between legal and illegal activity was blurred even more by privateering, a form of theft practiced since the 1500s. Privateering was legal, government-sanctioned piracy against enemy ships. If you were a British merchant captain and Britain was at war with France, you could get a special license from the crown to capture and plunder French ships. Privateering was a cheap and often lucrative way for the governments of the day to fight the enemy. Although it cost nothing to issue a license for stealing enemy ships, there was a drawback. Privateering trained some ship captains in piracy. They became good at plundering enemy ships and developed a taste for it. When the war was over and it was no longer legal to prey on foreign ships, some of these captains and their crews often continued plundering. They graduated from privateers to pirates.

And some of them became less particular about their targets and practiced piracy on any ship that carried a tempting cargo, even ships of their own nation.

Another reason piracy was tolerated by North Carolinians was that the pirates sold what they had stolen to the colonists at very reasonable rates. As a rule, contrary to popular myth, pirates did not find chests full of jewels and gold coins on the ships they plundered. They found trade goods, from guns and iron tools to kegs of rum and citrus fruits. The pirates then turned this loot into cash by selling it off to colonists looking for cheap, tax-free goods. Some of the wealthiest and most powerful people in the colony made their money by buying the pirates' booty and reselling it to other colonists at a higher price.

A final reason why piracy was so common in the waters around North Carolina was geography. Pirates needed places to hide their ships, and the Outer Banks, with its shifting sands and shallow sounds, provided an ideal refuge.

Blackbeard

The most notorious of North Carolina's pirates was Blackbeard. Edward Teach, alias Thatch, alias Blackbeard, was born in Bristol, England, probably in 1680. Blackbeard was typical of those who graduated from privateering to piracy. Operating out of Jamaica during Queen Anne's War (a war among Britain, France, and Spain fought in Europe and North America from 1702 to 1713), Blackbeard was a legal British privateer, preying on Spanish and French ships. When the war ended in 1713, he moved his headquarters to New Providence Island in the Bahamas and continued to rob ships. In 1718, the British drove the pirate from the Bahamas, and Blackbeard brought his whole crew to the North

The November 22, 1718 capture of the infamous pirate Blackbeard by the Royal Navy at Ocracoke Inlet off the Virginia coast is depicted above in this nineteenth-century painting by Jean Leon Gerome Ferris. In order to make his appearance more terrifying and weaken the courage of his enemies, Blackbeard would weave hemp into his hair and set it on fire during battle. During the battle that led to his capture, Blackbeard was reportedly shot five times and received more than twenty sword cuts. After dying of his wounds, Blackbeard was beheaded by the Royal Navy captain and his head hung in the ship's rigging. The report of Blackbeard's capture and death is reported at bottom in an article from the March 2, 1719 issue of the *Boston News-Letter*, at that time the only newspaper in the American colonies.

Carolina coast. Blackbeard himself went to live freely and openly in the North Carolina town of Bath.

Blackbeard and his men preyed on British and colonial ships all along the Carolina coast. A British expedition was sent to destroy Blackbeard and his operation, but the pirate escaped to Bath with a rich cargo that he had captured from a French ship.

Blackbeard benefited from the corruption of Carolina's colonial government. Tobias Knight, the secretary of Governor Charles Eden, let Blackbeard store some of his booty in Knight's barn. When some angry North Carolinians searched Knight's property and proved that this had occurred, Governor Eden protested this "unlawful and improper action" taken by the colonists. Soon afterward, some colonists broke into Knight's house to examine the public records for proof that both he and Eden were helping Blackbeard. The governor had them arrested for breaking and entering.

Stede Bonnet

Another well-known figure during the heyday of piracy in North Carolina was Stede Bonnet, a man of wealth and education who is remembered as the "gentleman pirate." For a time, after retiring from the British army, Bonnet lived in comfort on a Barbados estate and was known as a respectable man. No one knows why he abandoned his role as gentleman farmer and turned to piracy, but in 1717, he joined Blackbeard's gang. He then launched his own career as a pirate, taking North Carolina's Lower Cape Fear as his base of operations.

Eventually, both Blackbeard and Bonnet met their demise at the hands of the law (although not the corrupt government that was in charge of North Carolina at the time). Earlier, in 1712, North and South Carolina, once jointly governed, began to be

The reasons behind Stede Bonnet's decision to abandon his comfortable life as a sugar plantation owner are unclear. Bonnet never explained why he became a pirate, but historians have suggested several possibilities. Some think he was mentally ill, while others think he was simply bored with his comfortable but predictable life. The popular legend claims that Bonnet set sail in order to escape a nagging wife. Upon his capture in 1718, Bonnet begged for his life, offering to have all of his limbs cut off to guarantee that he would never again engage in piracy. This strange offer was refused, and Bonnet was hanged on December 10, 1718.

ruled by separate colonial governments. Fed up with Bonnet's attacks on his colony's shipping, South Carolina governor Robert Johnson sent an expedition against Bonnet headed by Colonel William Rhett. Meeting Bonnet in the Cape Fear River, Rhett's forces captured the pirate after a furious five-hour battle. Bonnet was taken to Charleston, South Carolina, where he was tried and convicted of piracy. On December 10, 1718, he was hanged along with twenty-nine other pirates.

Meanwhile, a few weeks after Bonnet's capture, Governor Alexander Spotswood of the Virginia colony sent out two ships in search of Blackbeard. The vessels were commanded by Lieutenant Robert Maynard of the Royal Navy. On November 22, 1718, Maynard met Blackbeard near Ocracoke Inlet and killed the pirate along with half his crew of eighteen. The remaining nine members of Blackbeard's crew were taken to Virginia, where they were tried and hanged. Although occasional later outbreaks of piracy surfaced on the Carolina coast, it was never again the scourge it had been in its brief golden age.

CHAPTER 4

Though the colorful and violent early history of North Carolina is often what gets emphasized and retold, most North Carolinians did not spend their days warring with Native Americans or buying illegal goods from pirates. Instead, they spent their long, hard days wresting a living from a land that required but also rewarded tireless work. Like most of North America's European inhabitants during the colonial period, the people of North Carolina devoted the largest portion of their energies to farming.

Life in Colonial North Carolina

Farming in North Carolina

The earliest European settlers in North America brought Old World crops with them to America. Some of these, such as olives, silk, and French grapes, did not take kindly to the soil and climate of North Carolina. Other European imports such as wheat, oats, and rice were much more successful. In the long run, though, settlers in North Carolina had their greatest success with the same crops that Native Americans had developed over the course of thousands of years of selective breeding: corn (at first called Indian corn, since "corn" is the word for all grain in Britain), beans, peas, white potatoes, sweet potatoes, and tobacco.

The habit of smoking and sniffing American-grown tobacco had been introduced to Europe by Sir Walter Raleigh as part of his plan to promote the settlement of his Roanoke colony. The habit took hold, and tobacco quickly became the major cash crop of

When settlers first migrated from Virginia to North Carolina after 1655, they had trouble growing crops in the region's dry, sandy soil. Luckily, tobacco grows well in thin soil, and there was a strong market for the product in England. After 1725, groups of Germans, Scots, and Welsh began to settle in Carolina and grow tobacco, a crop with which they were already familiar. The above image of slaves rolling dried tobacco leaves on a plantation dates from this time period. Initially, North Carolina's tobacco industry was kept very small by the dominance of Virginia growers. By 1880, however, there were 126 tobacco factories in North Carolina. Annually, they produced 6.5 million pounds of chewing tobacco, 4 million pounds of smoking tobacco, and several million rolled cigarettes. In 1884, the factory of W. Duke, Sons and Company in Durham began operating a cigarette-rolling machine that could roll 120,000 cigarettes a day.

North Carolina. North Carolina's farmers became experts at growing and curing tobacco. When the leaves had been air-cured or sun-cured, they were packed into giant barrels called hogsheads that weighed anywhere from 800 to 2,000 pounds (363 to 907 kilograms). Then they were shipped to England.

When European settlers first came to America, wild animals were abundant, but livestock was in short supply. Skilled hunters had no trouble getting meat, but farmers did not find it so easy. It took a while for the settlers to change this, but the farms eventually became populated by horses, cattle, and hogs. Razorback hogs provided most of the colonists' meat. When the settlers were ready to slaughter, great droves of hogs were driven on foot to markets in Virginia or even as far away as Pennsylvania.

Today, one thinks of cattle drives as a feature of the American West, but there was a time when colonial North Carolina was also a major beef producer. The methods used to raise cattle were similar to those used later during the heyday of Western ranching. For example, the cattle of North Carolina were branded to discourage stealing. There were also annual cattle roundups that were followed by long cattle drives to beef markets in Charleston, Virginia, and Philadelphia and Lancaster, Pennsylvania.

Industry in North Carolina

Often living far away from the places where goods were sold, North Carolina's frontiersmen were rich in land but poor in cash. As such, they had to be versatile and self-sufficient. Farmers did not only have to master the science of raising crops and livestock. In order to survive, they also had to be trappers, hunters, engineers, carpenters, mechanics, and businesspeople. A farmer's wife and children had to work the land with him, make cloth with the help of spinning wheels and looms, and stitch together animal hides into shoes, breeches, and other articles of clothing. Most colonists grew virtually all of their own food and made their own soap, candles, furniture, farm tools, and household utensils.

During the colonial era, pine trees were a central element in North Carolina's economy. One of the colony's most common trees, pines, provided resin, turpentine, and timber. These products are known as "naval stores" because they were used by merchants and navies for the construction and maintenance of their ships. The pine tree is so important to North Carolina's history and economy that it was designated the official state tree in 1963. In the nineteenth-century engraving above, a turpentine distillery sits nestled amid a pine forest as a wagonload of turpentine heads off to market. Turpentine is produced by collecting pine sap and heating it with water. What remains after this distillation is turpentine.

Household and agricultural labor was not the only kind of industry in the colony, however. Colonial North Carolina developed two major industries—naval stores and lumber products. Naval stores were needed for use in shipbuilding and ship maintenance. These were vital commodities since the shipping industry was the basis of colonial trade and the foundation upon which the British Empire was built. The most important of these naval products were tar, pitch, rosin, and turpentine, all available in plentiful supply from the virgin pine forests of North Carolina. From 1720 to 1870, North Carolina led the world in the production of naval stores. Seven-eighths of the tar, one-half of the turpentine, and one-fifth of the pitch exported to England from all of its American colonies came from North Carolina. North Carolina is called the Tar Heel State because of all the tar it exported to England in colonial times.

Lumber was an even greater source of cash for the colony. North Carolina was a land blanketed by forest. The need for lumber throughout America was enormous as the colonies grew, developed, and continued to build outward. The need was great in England, too, which was already largely deforested by the eighteenth century. By the early 1700s, water-powered sawmills had sprung up throughout North Carolina to help meet the ever-growing demand for lumber.

CHAPTER 5

Throughout the 1700s, the American colonies grew more and more estranged from Britain, mostly over the issues of high taxes, Parliament's intrusion into colonial affairs, and the colonists' lack of representation in Parliament. Eventually they declared their independence and fought a war with their mother country to obtain the right to govern themselves.

Taxation Without Representation

During the first half of the 1700s, the colonies benefited from what historians call the "salutary neglect" of the mother country. That is, the British government did not pay very much attention to the colonies, and the colonies were better off as a result. Far from the watchful eye of Britain, the colonies were allowed to govern themselves and develop their own institutions. In addition, the trade restrictions Britain imposed on its colonies were not strictly enforced, giving the Americans an opportunity to develop industries, trade relationships, and wealth.

The Road to Revolution

In 1763, however, Britain renewed its interest in the colonies with its New Colonial Policy. At the time, the British had just won a war against the French, fought in both Europe (in what became known as the Seven Years' War) and North America (where it was called the French and Indian War). By war's end, the British and their American colonists had driven the French from North America and added four new colonies—Quebec, East Florida, West Florida, and Grenada—to Britain's possessions in the New World.

War is always an expensive venture, and the British now needed money to help meet military expenses. They felt that it was time for the colonies to start contributing to the costs of their own defense. The resulting policy changes required the colonies to pay taxes on goods they bought from Britain. In addition, colonists would be required to trade exclusively with Britain—as they were supposed to have been doing all along. What was the use of having colonies at all, the British reasoned, if the Americans bought their cloth, tools, sugar, and tea from the merchants of France and Holland? To the British at the time, the answer seemed self-evident. Colonies existed only to enrich the mother country.

In 1765, the British parliament went even further by passing the Stamp Act, which required colonists to use stamped paper for many types of legal documents and pay a tax to Britain for every stamp. The Stamp Act led to angry protests in all of the original thirteen colonies, including North Carolina. The British were surprised by the American reaction because the tax was smaller than a similar levy that British subjects had to pay at home. But to the colonists, there was more at stake than this one small tax. The Americans believed they were being taxed by a Parliament that did not represent their concerns and interests, since the colonies did not have the ability to elect members of Parliament. The divide between the mother country and its colonies grew, as Britain's callous disregard stoked the Americans' anger. Many colonists began to grow more vocal in their opposition to British colonial policy and in their support of independence.

The same year that the Stamp Act was passed, a North Carolinian named Maurice Moore published a pamphlet titled "The Justice and Policy of Taxing the American Colonies in Great Britain, Considered." The piece argued against Britain's right to tax the colonies. Like other American writers who opposed

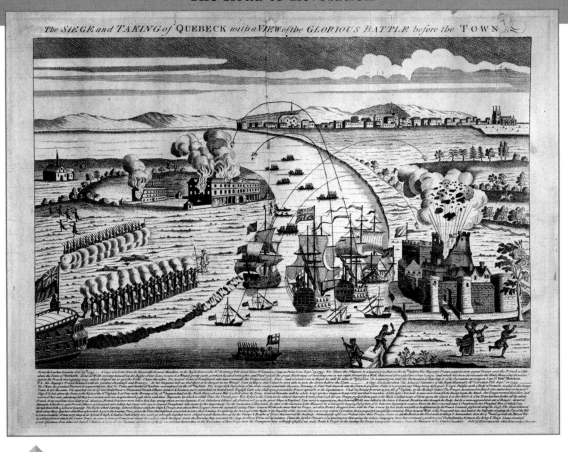

The three-month-long Siege of Quebec—a large settlement and garrison in the French colony of Canada, or New France—was the largest and the single most important battle of the French and Indian War. This war was the North American extension of the Seven Years War in Europe between England and France. When the French also lost Detroit and Montreal to the British in 1760, the two European powers' rivalry in the New World came to an end. As the French colonial presence in North America came to an end, so too did the French and Indian War. The Treaty of Paris, signed on February 10, 1763, gave all of North America east of the Mississippi, other than New Orleans, to the British. The French turned over their claims of New Orleans and the lands west of the Mississippi to Spain. A contemporary depiction of the siege and capture of Quebec appears above.

the Stamp Act, Moore noted that the colonists could legally be taxed only with their own consent. This meant that they must have some representation in Parliament to allow them to vote for or against the taxes.

John Penn

Will Hooper

Joseph Hewes

Pictured above are the three men who signed the Declaration of Independence as representatives of North Carolina. Strangely enough, none of these men was actually from North Carolina. Each of them moved there as an adult. Will Hooper was born in Massachusetts and graduated from Harvard College before working as a lawyer in North Carolina. John Penn was a self-educated lawyer who was born in Virginia and moved to North Carolina to practice law. Joseph Hewes was born in Princeton, New Jersey, and attended Princeton College. He established a shipping business in North Carolina and became rich.

The British eventually repealed the Stamp Act, but Parliament kept looking for ways to raise money from the colonies. In 1773, the passage of the Tea Act led to a protest in which the citizens of Boston threw £15,000 of East India Company tea into Boston Harbor. This would become popularly known as the Boston Tea Party. The British responded by closing the Port of Boston. They sought to punish Boston by preventing needed supplies from reaching the city. North Carolinians observed that "the cause of Boston is the cause of all." To help the Bostonians hold out against the British embargo, they sent a ship with corn flour and pork to an open port north of Boston in Salem, Massachusetts.

Rebellion, Independence, and Statehood

In 1774, colonists had reached such a pitch of anger and frustration that they began looking for a way to unite in opposition to the British. They decided to call together a Continental Congress—a meeting of representatives from all the colonies—to gather in Philadelphia, Pennsylvania. North Carolinians elected William Hooper, Richard Caswell, and Joseph Hewes as delegates to the Continental Congress. North Carolina's royal governor, Josiah Martin, who was appointed by the king of England, tried to prevent North Carolina from joining the other colonies in opposition to Britain. He urged North Carolinians to resist "the monster, sedition [rebellion] which has dared to raise his impious [unreligious] head in America," as quoted by Lefler. His plea went unanswered.

Governor Martin had lost control of the colony. In late May 1775, five weeks after the American Revolution began in Massachusetts, he fled the governor's mansion. On June 2, Martin arrived at Fort Johnston on Cape Fear. Learning that North

North Carolina   In Congress 12th April 1776

The Select Committee to take into Consideration the Usurpations and Violences attempted and Committed by the King and Parliament of Britain against America, and the further Measures to be taken for frustrating the Same, and for the better defence of this Province, reported as follows, towit.

It appears to your Committee that pursuant to the plan concerted by the British Ministry for subjugating America, the King and Parliament of Great Britain have usurped a power over the persons and properties of the people unlimited and uncontrouled. And disregarding their humble petitions for peace Liberty and Safety, have made divers Legislative Acts denouncing War, Famine and every Species of Calamity against the Continent in General. That British Fleets and Armies have been and still are daily employed in destroying the people, and committing the most horid devastations on the Country. ——

That

On April 4, 1776, North Carolina's Fourth Provincial Congress assembled in Halifax, North Carolina, to discuss the grievances of its colonists against the increasingly tyrannical British rule. The complaints included Britain's disregard of the American colonies' repeated pleas for peace and liberty, and the disruption of and interference with the colonies' trade and commerce. Their discussions and deliberations resulted in a document called the Halifax Resolves. The Halifax Resolves was the first formal and official statement by an American colony in favor of independence and complete separation from Britain. See the transcription on page 54.

Carolina militiamen were about to attack, he took refuge aboard a British ship. He did so just in time, for on July 19, the North Carolina militia burned down Fort Johnston.

In North Carolina, as in the other colonies, the outbreak of war made reconciliation with the British far less likely. Independence began to seem like a real possibility rather than the angry talk of overtaxed colonists blowing off steam. On April 12, 1776, North Carolina's Fourth Provincial Congress adopted the Halifax Resolves, stating: "Resolved: That the delegates for this Colony in the Continental Congress be impowered to concur with the delegates of the other Colonies in declaring Indpendency . . ."

On July 4, 1776, North Carolina delegates William Hooper, Joseph Hewes, and John Penn signed the Declaration of Independence, the document that officially notified England's King George III, the British parliament, and the entire world that the thirteen American colonies were separating from Britain to become an independent nation—the United States of America. In November and December of that year, North Carolina's Provincial Congress met to form its first constitution. North Carolina's history as a British colony was officially over. Its history as an American state had begun.

TIMELINE

1524 —— Giovanni da Verrazano explores the North Carolina coast.

1540 —— Spanish explorer Hernando de Soto reaches the mountains of southwestern North Carolina.

1585 —— The first British colony in the New World is founded on Roanoke Island.

1587 —— A second colony is founded on Roanoke. Virginia Dare is born, the first child of British parents born in America. This colony disappears, becoming known as the "lost colony."

1607 —— The first permanent British colony is founded in Jamestown, Virginia.

1657 —— Nathaniel Batts settles in North Carolina, the colony's first-known permanent white settler.

1663 —— King Charles II signs a charter making eight of his supporters "the true and absolute lords proprietors" of Carolina.

1669 —— The lords proprietors issue the Fundamental Constitutions of Carolina, planning to run the colony according to a feudal system.

1711 —— War begins between the Tuscarora Indians and white colonists and their Native American allies.

1717 —— Hard economic times in Ulster, Ireland, lead to the first wave of Scotch-Irish immigration to America.

1718 —— The pirate Blackbeard is killed near Ocracoke Inlet in North Carolina.

1746 —— Scotland rebels against British rule and is defeated at the Battle of Culloden. In the aftermath of the war, many Scottish Highlanders immigrate to North America.

1753 —— Moravian settlers from Bethlehem, Pennsylvania, arrive in Wachovia, North Carolina.

1754 —— The French and Indian War (1754–1763), fought between the French and British, their respective colonists, and their various Native American allies, begins.

1774 —— North Carolina's First Provincial Congress chooses delegates to the First Continental Congress.

1776 —— North Carolina's Fourth Provincial Congress at Halifax authorizes North Carolina delegates in the Continental Congress to "concur in independency" from Britain. North Carolina becomes the first state to vote in favor of independence. The Battle of Moores Creek Bridge is the first battle of the American Revolution to be fought in North Carolina.

1789 —— North Carolina becomes the twelfth state of the United States of America. The University of North Carolina is chartered, becoming the first public school in the United States.

1861 —— North Carolina secedes from the United States in advance of the Civil War.

1868 —— North Carolina is readmitted to the Union after the end of the Civil War in which 40,000 of its soldiers died.

PRIMARY SOURCE TRANSCRIPTIONS

Page 10: Excerpt of Charter to Sir Walter Raleigh, 1584

Transcription
Elizabeth, by the Grace of God, etc. To all people to whom these presents shall come, greeting:

Know ye, that, of our especial grace, certain science, and mere motion, we have given and granted, and, by these presents, for us, our heirs and successors, do give and grant, to our trusty and well-beloved servant, Walter Raleighe, Esquire, and to his heirs and assigns, forever, free liberty and license from time to time, and at all times forever hereafter, to discover, search, find out, and view such remote heathen and barbarous Lands, Countries, and territories, not actually possessed of any Christian Prince and inhabited by Christian people, as to him, his heirs and assigns, and to every or any of them, shall seem good; and the same to have, hold, occupy, and enjoy, to him, his heirs and assigns, forever; with all prerogatives, commodities, jurisdictions, and royalties, privileges, Franchises, and pre-eminences, there or thereabouts, both by sea and land, whatsoever we, by our letters patents, may grant, and as we, or any of our noble Progenitors, have heretofore granted to any person or persons, bodies politic or corporate.

Page 15: Excerpt from the Charter of Carolina, March 24, 1663

Transcription
CHARLES the Second, by the grace of God, king of England, Scotland, France, and Ireland, Defender of the Faith, &c., To all to whom these present shall come: Greeting:

. . . Know ye, therefore, that we, favouring the pious and noble purpose of the said Edward Earl of Clarendon, George Duke of

Albemarle, William Lord Craven, John Lord Berkley, Anthony Lord Ashley, Sir George Carteret, Sir William Berkley, and Sir John Colleton, of our special grace, certain knowledge and meer motion, have given, granted atoll confirmed, and by this our present charter, for us, our heirs and successors, do give, grant and confirm unto the said Edward Earl of Clarendon, George Duke of Albemarle, William Lord Craven, Atolls Lord Berkley, Anthony Lord Ashley, Sir George Carteret, Sir William Berkley, and Sir John Colleton, their heirs and assigns, all that territory or tract of ground, scituate, lying and being within our dominions of America, extending from the north end of the island called Lucke island, which lieth in the southern Virginia seas, and within six and thirty degrees of the northern latitude, and to the west as far as the south seas, and so southerly as far as the river St. Matthias, which bordereth upon the coast of Florida, and within one and thirty degrees of northern latitude, and so west in a direct line as far as the south seas aforesaid; together with all and singular ports, harbours, bays, rivers, isles and islets belonging to the country aforesaid; and also all the soil, lands, fields, woods, mountlills, fields, lakes, rivers, bays and islets, scituate or being within the bounds or limits aforesaid, with the fishing of all sorts of fish, whales, sturgeons and all other royal fishes in the sea, bays, islets and rivers within the premises, and the fish therein taken; and moreover all veins, mines, quarries, as well discovered as not discovered, of gold, silver, gems, precious stones, and all other whatsoever, be it of stones, metals, or any other thing whatsoever, found or to be found within the countries, isles and limits aforesaid.

Page 48: The Halifax Resolves, April 12, 1776

Transcription

The Select Committee taking into Consideration the usurpations and violences attempted and committed by the King and Parliament of Britain against America, and the further Measures to be taken for frustrating the same, and for the better defence of this province reported as follows, to wit,

It appears to your Committee that pursuant to the Plan concerted by the British Ministry for subjugating America, the King and Parliament of Great Britain have usurped a Power over the Persons and Properties of the People unlimited and uncontrouled and disregarding their humble Petitions for Peace, Liberty and safety, have made divers Legislative Acts, denouncing War Famine and every Species of Calamity daily employed in destroying the People and committing the most horrid devastations on the Country. That Governors in different Colonies have declared Protection to Slaves who should imbrue their Hands in the Blood of their Masters. That the Ships belonging to America are declared prizes of War and many of them have been violently seized and confiscated in consequence of which multitudes of the people have been destroyed or from easy Circumstances reduced to the most Lamentable distress.
And whereas the moderation hitherto manifested by the United Colonies and their sincere desire to be reconciled to the mother Country on Constitutional Principles, have procured no mitigation of the aforesaid Wrongs and usurpations and no hopes remain of obtaining redress by those Means alone which have been hitherto tried, Your Committee are of Opinion that the house should enter into the following Resolve, to wit

Resolved that the delegates for this Colony in the Continental Congress be impowered to concur with the other delegates of the other Colonies in declaring Independency, and forming foreign Alliances, resolving to this Colony the Sole, and Exclusive right of forming a Constitution and Laws for this Colony, and of appointing delegates from time to time (under the direction of a general Representation thereof to meet the delegates of the other Colonies for such purposes as shall be hereafter pointed out.

GLOSSARY

British Commonwealth A political organization of nations that were once British colonies and were loyal to the British monarch.

Catholic Church The body of Christians who accept the leadership of the pope. In the Middle Ages, all European Christians were Catholic. After the Reformation, those who broke away from the pope became known as Protestants.

charter A contract that guarantees rights and privileges, especially a contract issued to a city or colony by the government of a country.

colony A group of people living in a new territory but retaining ties to the parent nation.

harbor A part of a body of water near land that is deep and sheltered enough to allow ships to anchor.

Highlanders Inhabitants of the hills and mountains of central and northern Scotland.

lords proprietors High-ranking men given a charter by King Charles II of England to rule the colony of Carolina.

Moravians Members of a Protestant denomination deriving from a fifteenth-century religious reform movement in Bohemia and Moravia (in what is the modern-day Czech Republic).

navigator A person expert at charting the course of ships and piloting them to their destinations.

Palatines People originally from the upper Rhine area of Germany.

Presbyterian Church One of the Protestant Church denominations, governed by ministers and elders of the congregation.

privateer An armed, private ship licensed by a government to attack enemy shipping.

Protestant A member of any of several Christian denominations that deny the authority of the pope and support the Reformation principles first put forth by sixteenth-century religious leaders such as Martin Luther and John Calvin, who broke away from the Catholic Church.

Quakers Members of the Society of Friends, a Christian sect that rejects sacraments and ordained ministers and opposes war.

Reformation The religious reform movement that began in the early sixteenth century, when many people began to question the beliefs and practices of the Catholic Church.

Scots-Irish The Scottish settlers of Northern Ireland and their descendants. Also referred to as Scotch-Irish.

sedition Resistance to or rebellion against lawful authority.

smuggling Illegal importation or exportation, especially without paying import or export taxes.

FOR MORE INFORMATION

Federation of North Carolina Historical Societies
4610 Mail Service Center
Raleigh, NC 27699-4610
(919) 807-7280
Web site: http://www.ah.dcr.state.nc.us/affiliates/fnchs/fnchs.htm

North Carolina Museum of History
4650 Mail Service Center
Raleigh, NC 27699-4650
(919) 807-7900
Web site: http://ncmuseumofhistory.org

State Library of North Carolina
Archives and History
State Library Building
109 East Jones Street
Raleigh, NC 27601
(919) 807-7450
Web site: http://statelibrary.dcr.state.nc.us

Web Sites

Due to the changing nature of Internet links, the Rosen Publishing Group, Inc., has developed an online list of Web sites related to the subject of this book. This site is updated regularly. Please use this link to access the list:

http://www.rosenlinks.com/pstc/noca

FOR FURTHER READING

Barrett, Tracy. *Growing Up in Colonial America*. Brookfield, CT: Millbrook Press, 1995.

Carlson, Laurie. *Colonial Kids*. Chicago, IL: Chicago Review Press, 1997.

Carter, Alden R. *The Colonial Wars: Clashes in the Wilderness*. New York, NY: Scholastic Library Publishing, 1993.

Hakim, Joy. *Making Thirteen Colonie*s (A History of US), Vol. 2, 3rd ed. New York, NY: Oxford University Press, 2002.

Hermes, Patricia. *Our Strange New Land: Elizabeth's Diary Jamestown Virginia, 1607*. New York, NY: Scholastic, 2000.

Howorth, Sarah. *Colonial People*. Brookfield, CT: Millbrook Press, 1994.

Maestro, Betsy. *The New Americans: Colonial Times 1620–1689*. New York, NY: Harper Trophy, 2004.

Masoff, Joy. *Colonial Times 1600–1700* (Chronicle of America). New York, NY: Scholastic, 2000.

Rafle, Sarah. *North Carolina: The Tar Heel State*. Milwaukee, WI: Gareth Stevens Publishing, 2002.

Sateren, Shelley Swanson. *North Carolina Facts and Symbols*. Mankato, MN: Bridgestone Books, 2003.

Weintraub, Aileen. *Blackbeard: Eighteenth-Century Pirate of the Spanish Main and the Carolina Coast*. New York, NY: PowerKids Press, 2002.

Whitehurst, Susan. *The Colony of North Carolina*. New York, NY: PowerKids Press, 2000.

BIBLIOGRAPHY

Aronson, Marc. *Sir Walter Raleigh and the Quest for El Dorado*. New York, NY: Clarion, 2001.

Butler, Lindley S., and Alan D. Watson. *The North Carolina Experience: An Interpretive and Documentary Approach*. Chapel Hill, NC: University of North Carolina Press, 1984.

Butler, Lindley S. *Pirates, Privateers, and Rebels of the Carolina Coast*. Chapel Hill, NC: University of North Carolina Press, 2000.

Fritz, Jean. *The Lost Colony of Roanoke*. New York, NY: G. P. Putnam & Sons, 2004.

Lee, E. Lawrence Jr. *The Indian Wars in North Carolina, 1663–1763*. Raleigh, NC: Carolina Charter Tercentenary Commission, 1963.

Lefler, Hugh Talmage, and William S. Powell. *Colonial North Carolina: A History*. New York, NY: Charles Scribners Sons, 1973.

Lefler, Hugh Talmage. *North Carolina: The History of a Southern State*. Chapel Hill, NC: University of North Carolina Press, 1973.

Marrin, Albert. *Struggle for a Continent: The French and Indian Wars, 1690–1760*. New York, NY: Atheneum, 1987.

Powell, William S. *North Carolina: A Bicentennial History*. New York, NY: W. W. Norton & Company, 1977.

Powell, William S. *North Carolina: A History*. Chapel Hill, NC: University of North Carolina Press, 1988.

Powell, William S. *North Carolina Through Four Centuries*. Chapel Hill, NC: University of North Carolina Press, 1989.

Stick, David. *The Graveyard of the Atlantic*. Chapel Hill, NC: University of North Carolina Press, 1952.

PRIMARY SOURCE IMAGE LIST

Page 5: A 1594 color engraving of Christopher Columbus by Theodore de Bry, housed in the Kunstbibliothek, Staatliche Museen zu Berlin, Berlin, Germany.

Page 7: A circa 1540 woodcut print map of the New World by Sebastian Münster.

Page 10 (left): The 1584 Charter to Sir Walter Raleigh, issued by Queen Elizabeth I, housed in the Public Record Office, London, England.

Page 10 (right): A circa sixteenth-century portrait of Sir Walter Raleigh by an anonymous artist. Housed in the National Portrait Gallery of Ireland, Dublin, Ireland.

Page 12: A circa sixteenth-century lithograph entitled *Indians Dancing*, by John White.

Page 15: The Charter of 1663, issued by Charles II, king of England, granting the province of Carolina to eight lords proprietors. Housed in the North Carolina State Archives, Raleigh, North Carolina.

Page 18: A map of the New Bern settlement made by Baron Christopher von Graffenried in October 1710.

Page 21: A circa 1750 "Gaelic Charm" written mostly in Gaelic and once belonging to Dougald McFarland of Moore County (later Cumberland County), North Carolina. Housed in the North Carolina Archives.

Page 22: A circa nineteenth-century illustrated family record (fraktur) for Philip Sell of North Carolina. Housed in the Old Military and Civil Records division of the National Archives Building, Washington, D.C.

Page 24: Two woodcuts from the 1849 edition of *The Life and Adventures of Henry Bibb*.

Page 27: A circa 1711 sketch by Baron Christoph von Graffenried of the Tuscarora capture of John Lawson, von Graffenried, and a black slave. Housed in the Burgerbibliothek in Bern, Switzerland.

Page 28: A late sixteenth-century watercolor portrait of a Secotan or Pomeiooc Indian by John White. Housed in the British Museum, London, England.

Page 31: An August 4, 1697, letter from Lords Commissioners of the Council of Trade to Mr. Basse Sr. concerning piracy in the American colonies, sent from Whitehall, London, England.

Page 34 (bottom): A newspaper article on the capture of the pirate Blackbeard appearing in the *Boston News-Letter* on March 2, 1719.

Page 39: A 1725 scene from an American tobacco plantation, from the book *A Compleat History of Drugs*, by A. Pomet, published in London, England, in 1725.

Page 41: A circa 1850 engraving of a turpentine distillery by Frederick Law Olmsted, from his 1856 book *A Journey in the Seaboard Slave States*.

Page 45: A 1759 print entitled *The Siege and Taking of Quebeck*. Housed in the National Archives of Canada, in Ottawa, Canada.

Page 48: The Halifax Resolves, submitted on April 12, 1776. Housed in the National Archives, Washington, D.C.

INDEX

Index

About the Author

Phillip Margulies is a writer who lives in New York City. He has a keen interest in American history and has written extensively on various aspects of it, especially colonial and revolutionary history.

Photo Credits

Cover Giraudon/Art Resource, NY; p. 1 © The Mariners' Museum; p. 5 Bildarchiv Preussischer Kulturbesitz/Art Resource, NY; p. 7 Library of Congress Geography and Map Division; pp. 10 (left), 15, 21 (right), 27 North Carolina State Archives; p. 10 (right) Anonymous/National Portrait Gallery of Ireland, Dublin, Ireland/http://www.bridgeman.co.uk; p. 12 White, John (after)/Private Collection/http://www.bridgeman.co.uk; p. 18 Tryon Palace Historic Sites & Gardens; p. 21 (left) City of Edinburgh Museums and Art Galleries, Scotland/http://www.bridgeman.co.uk; pp. 22, 48 National Archives; p. 24 Special Collections Department, J.Y. Joyner Library, East Carolina University, Greenville, NC; p. 28 HIP/Scala/Art Resource, NY; p. 31 U.S. History, Local History and Genealogy, The New York Public Library, Astor, Lenox and Tilden Foundations; p. 34 (top) Private Collection/http://www.bridgeman.co.uk; (bottom) Rare Books Division, The New York Public Library, Astor Lenox and Tilden Foundations; p. 36 Library of Congress Rare Book & Special Collections; p. 39 © The Image Works; pp. 41, 46 North Carolina Collection, University of North Carolina Library at Chapel Hill; p. 45 Nation Archives of Canada/C-077769.

Photo Researcher: Amy Feinberg